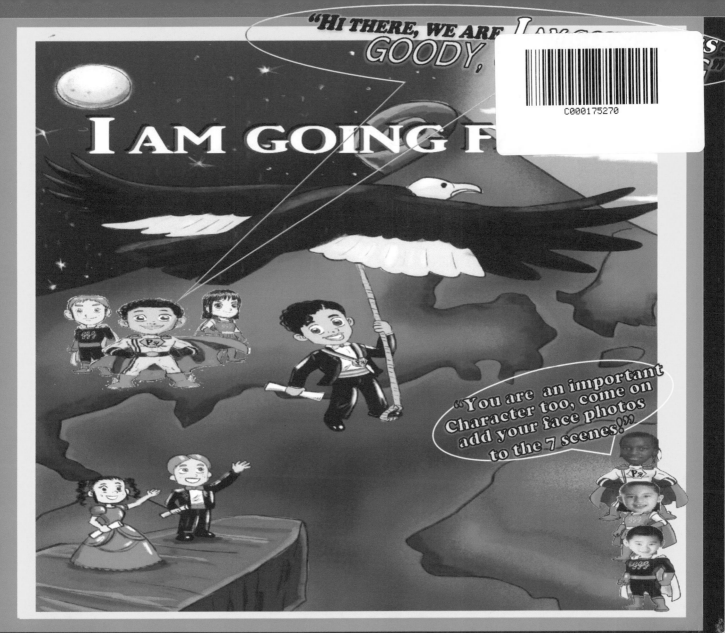

THIS REMASTERED BOOK BELONGS TO
YOUNG MASTER/S OR MISS/S

Received at age/s: ....6...........

From: ....

On: ....

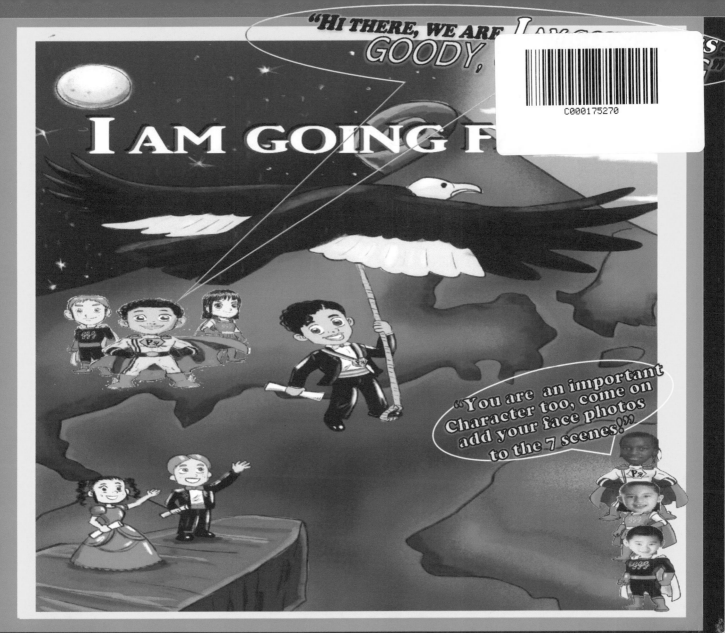

If lost & found please do the good thing *by calling this*
number..
arranging *Its* return to the child's parent or carer.

Thank you from CoJ Israel.

First Published June 2019 by IngramSpark Ltd,
1246 Heil Quaker Blvd, La Vergne, TN 3708 America.
On behalf of Self-Published British Author CJ Israel, previously
known as CJ Pohl of business name: I AM GOING FAR WITH MILES PR®
Registered business address: 61 Bridge Street, Kington, HR5 3DJ, England, UK.

Author CJ Israel's official website is: **www.iamgoingfar.com**

ISBN 978-1-9999338-6-9 (HB)
ISBN 978-1-9999338-2-1 (PB)
ISBN 978-1-9999338-8-3 (eBook)
ISBN 978-1-9999338-9-0 (FUN ACTIVITY BOOKLET)

HEY THERE, FROM AUGUST 2021 ONWARDS LOOKOUT FOR THIS BOOK IN ARABIC!

ISBN 978-1-9999338-3-8 (HB) IN ARABIC
ISBN 978-1-9999338-4-5 (PB) IN ARABIC
ISBN 978-1-9999338-5-2 (eBook) IN ARABIC

Audiobooks, bedtime video reads & podcasts by me the author will also be available soon.

A CIP catalogue record for this book is available from the British library.

Printed and bound by IngramSpark®

7 DEDICATIONS & 1 MEMORIAL

To,
Almighty God the Creator,
You are the originator of my creativity and more, – in reverence, I humbly mirror the same belief you have in me, and I gladly give you ALL the glory back!

To my Mum
Ms. V S, When I was planted within the comfort of your tummy, God knew that I couldn't have asked for a greater Mummy. Thanks for everything mum. A billion kisses to you from me, your girl C. Xxx...

To
my youngest son, you gave me the ambition to join you on adventures, so I write to make our lives right. Thanks & be Good!

To ALL the Children out there, throughout this beautiful world. With love and the best of intentions for you, I, C J Isreal wrote and remastered this book. You see in life, be sure to know that it is good to practice doing things over again to get it just right. Improvement is part of learning to be your best. If at first you don't succeed-
'Try, try
and try again!'

To Meg & Harry,
Keep fighting for what is right. Pray to the Most-High God, each and every day and night. Never lose hope or sight. Receive the vision, to always make blessed decisions.

To,
My Father A M, Yahu, Fuad Sy Hasan, Gee, Detrick mee 2d, J Jules, Steve Harvey, Spike Lee, G Richards, General Levy, Kevin Campbell, Denzel Washington, Shak, Azari & R C Compton – greetings, gentlemen.
With warm affection, I salute you in saying the following –

"FROM THE SLUM WE **may have** COME, BUT WE... AINT DUMB!"
Men, of inspiration, keep being the Positive Role Models you are, our sons & daughters **need You!**

To My prayerful Sistrines & Brethrines, throughout the world, Quabna, Petrina, Shareen, Kamaria, Pauline, Pastor Harvey, Dee, Lil, Joyce, Elayne, Mish, Debs, Melania, Joe, Janet, Jackie & Neyney. Hold True & Fast to the Faith! xxxx

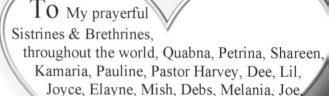

To, Papa Horst,
My family can never forget you!
May 17th, 1939 – May 20th, 2019

I AM GOING FAR

AUTHOR C J ISRAEL, ILLUSTRATED BY FUAD SY HASSAN

The remastered 1st book released April 2021.

PRINTED BY INGRAM SPARKS

'Hi
There,

It's **NICE** to meet **You!**
My **Mum** and **Dad** said they travelled
great distances and to faraway places,
to arrive at a perfect name for me.
I'm sure you'll agree they picked
the right one. Here's a short riddle to make you giggle -
Is my name short or is it long? Join me in a name guessing
introduction game. Here's a clue, and no my name doesn't
rhyme with the word...

shoe.

It does with **Smiles**. Can You Guess?

Yes, I'm...

Miles'.

What is your name?

New Friend/s, please write your name/s neatly on this dotted line!

PLEASE write it here **NICE** and clear because this Book is as much about **YOU**, as it is about **Me** and my close friends **Meg** and **Harry**.

Be sure to tell **EVERYONE** you see...

'I AM GOING FAR!'

YOU can come too although it might not be that easy to do.

Trekking through Jungles.

Climbing the steepest Mountains...

Running over lands, Hills then...

all the way to the **T**op.

across **D**eserts to the...

Diving the deepest Oceans that's sometimes where you will find me, with fellow divers **Meg** and **Harry**.
   As a brand-new member of our crew, we'll welcome and **salute YOU.** Your brother, sister, cousin or best **friend** can join us too.

"Politely ask a Grown-up helper to add a little DOUBLE-SIDED TAPE or Sticky Back Velcro to the RED CROSSES, sticking YOUR carefully cut-out FACE-PHOTO TO IT."

Pull your goggles on taking funny face photos!
Pick an AWESOME wetsuit to flipper swim our route.
High, dry and even slippery wet, we will go on
quests, as there is something important

EVERYONE SHOULD ...

KNOW.

"It may get **Tough** and rough being **d**aring as this, having to be **BRAVE** maybe sleeping in...

caves.

YOU SEE

In this BEAUTIFUL World...

8

We ALL have HOPES and DREAMS. As 'You, Meg and Harry can see, I, Miles, wants to do
REMARKABLE Things'.

That's why...

"I AM GOING FAR."

Sing the - I AM GOING FAR MARCHING SONG!

'JOIN us singing this Marching song!'
JOIN us singing this Marching song,
Repeat it to your friends, Repeat it to your FRIENDS!
'So, they can sing along - - Sing along - - Sing along - -
Sing along! SO, THEY CAN SING ALONG.'

^GET ready to ^be-e-come, ONE OF OUR CREW.
^GET ready to ^be-e-come, ONE OF OUR CREW.
Stand-up soldiers. Stand-up Backs STRAIGHT!
'STAND-UP. Backs STRAIGHT. Stand-up soldiers.
'Hurry Soldiers don't be late! Hurry Soldiers DON'T BE LATE,
DON'T BE LATE - DON'T BE LATE - DON'T BE LATE.'
^MARCH forward soldiers! ^MARCH-ING. Left, Right. SINGING

#Chorus

I am going far, I am going far, I am going far, I am going far,
With Miles PR, WITH MILES PR, WITH MILES PR AND THE -
'GOODY, GOODY GANG!'
I am going far, I am going far, I am going far,
'I am going far, with Miles PR, WITH MILES
PR, WITH MILES PR AND THE -
'GOODY. GOODY GANG!'

~End of Song~

"Politely ask a Grown-up
helper to add a little DOUBLE-SIDED TAPE
or Sticky Back Velcro to the PINK & BLUE, circles
sticking YOUR carefully cut-out FACE-PHOTO TO IT!"

We are going far it's true ....

You will be Going Far with close friends Meg, Harry and Me - 'Miles, on your side. Looking out for one another we'll be each other's guide, carefully making sure we don't slip or slide into trouble...

ONLY FOLLOW PEOPLE OF A GOOD EXAMPLE!

the best WE CAN BE.   Being ...OUR OWN

PERSONAL

BEST,

enables us to...

ENCOURAGE

other ...

CHILDREN'S...

'GREATNESS!'

Oh Yes, we're going far with Positive Role Model, **Miles PR'**.

On these adventures and trials, we will GLADLY go that EXTRA MILE WITH MILES. GIVING lots of GOOD things a TRY. REMEMBERING our MANNERS; saying – "HI, PLEASE, THANK YOU, SORRY OR... GOODBYE!"

HELPING other children become their BEST, is the Special **PR** emblem on Miles's chest. R looks up to positive P so much, that's why she turned around to take a second look. Now in case you never understood - P stands for Positive and R is for Role, and the person wearing Miles's emblem is the Model, so there you go... 'POSITIVE ROLE MODEL! 'We are LEARNING as we PLAY and SHARING what we find as these are BRILLIANT ways of us being . . .

KIND!

'Did you know that IT'S WRONG TO BULLY?

Saying mean things **isn't funny**. It's better to say nothing at all than to make someone upset and feel ...

"Politely ask a Grown-up helper to add a little **DOUBLE**-SIDED TAPE or Sticky Back Velcro to the PINK & BLUE Circles. Sticking YOUR carefully cut-out FACE-PHOTOS TO IT"

SMALL!'

15

'THE GOLDEN RULE is Don't be cruel'.
LOOK UP, not down with a frown, as
EXCELLENT BEHAVIOUR
deserves a...
CROWN!

'Just Like this Bird,

I AM GOING FAR, oh yes, I AM and with **You**, **Meg** and **Harry**, my GOODY, GOODY GANG by my side, we will look out for each other, always being GOOD GUIDES.

Now, I may not have a real beak to say - 'Tweet, Tweet' or sing songs... incredibly...

Sweet!

There's no real feathered vest upon **Miles's** chest.

There's no real winged jacket upon **Meg**, helping her soar the skies flying - North, South, East and West... All the same...WE'LL DO OUR BEST, TO **HELP** HER ACHIEVE AMAZING THINGS.

Dressed like a **Condor** or **Cockatoo**, squawking...

Yes, we do look ADORABLY cute - all dressed up in our SUPER FABULOUS, Tuxedo suits and GLAMOROUS dress to IMPRESS. Stylishly, standing out above the rest of V.I.P GUESTS. Now as **CONQUERORS** of various quests, we have done our **PERSONAL BEST**.

This evening we are receiving ☆POSITIVE ROLE MODEL☆ - MEDALS, CERTIFICATES and **AWARDS** and we are wondering if, we'll be KNIGHTED with a ...sword.

Although you may think I'm too small, and not that tall to drive MY black striped, yellow LAMBRO-GHINI car, with its radio turned up booming -"#WE ARE -WE ARE- GOING FAR!"

All the Same...

'**I** CAN SO, **I AM!**'

Hop into MY warmed seats Friends,

and never let this AWESOME ADVENTURE

of 'us' becoming our...

PERSONAL BEST, EVER...

"Go on children smile for the Cameras. Politely ask your grown-up helper to carefully stick your super fabulous, face-photos onto the blue & pink circles!"

28

End.

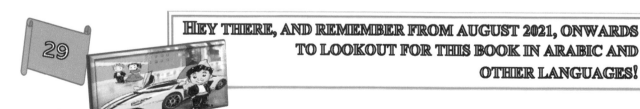

HEY THERE, AND REMEMBER FROM AUGUST 2021, ONWARDS TO LOOKOUT FOR THIS BOOK IN ARABIC AND OTHER LANGUAGES!

HIYA, I AM C J ISRAEL,

I remastered this book following my name change from C J Pohl in August of 2020.
Unconventional, Yes, I am and will always be, because life, is far too short to live it trying to be like someone else, so, I dare to be myself! We only get one chance to experience life, and I for, one, intend to live it well, meanwhile, empathising and encouraging you to do so too.

On the topic of achieving goals - I believe that great things are possible if you have FAITH, VISION and WORK HARD!

Investing my faith, in the belief that there is one Almighty Creator, I have chosen to be steadfast with my prayer to Him, and in doing so I have been blessed to work tirelessly on bringing my visions and ideas into reality. As an author/entrepreneur - I am a rebel with an almighty cause always.

MY MOTTO IS - IF AT FIRST YOU DON'T SUCCEED – TRY, TRY AND TRY PRAYING HARDER AGAIN... Originally, I wrote, launched and published part one of this book title – **I AM GOING FAR** in less than seven months of 2019. However, with it being my first-ever children's book of that which is intended to be a collection of aspirational; confidence-boosting, anti-bullying and healthy eating interactive books, I have since revised it a few times with the hope of it appealing even more so to the needs of - children, parents, carers and teachers.

"I BELIEVE IN MIRACLES AND DESTINY, SOME THINGS - ARE JUST MEANT TO BE!" Regarding this book's illustrations – 'well, despite speaking limited English my Indonesian illustrator having won my online art competition, he then busily went to work drawing in early 2019, creating these wonderful images from my hand drawn-sketches and written brief. At no time did he know what the storyline would be until he received a copy of this book.

A LITTLE MORE ABOUT ME...

I was born during the 1970s' in Manchester, England to church-going Jamaican parents, I think it is important to mention my background as being a mother of five, as I also am, we parents' often appreciate knowing about the influences propelling those potential influencers of our children and selves. For every action, there is a reaction, and for me aiming to be a fair and just person, treating people the way I would like to be treated is a major motivating factor in writing books that encourage greatness of nature - kindness and fairness. Over the years I have held numerous positions and titles, including Carnival Queen, as I love to dance, I also like to travel. Friends regard me as a fun-loving person that is a bit quirky but grounded too. You see in life we all do different things, sometimes out of the ordinary and I am no exception to that!

As a self-taught writer/author, designer and entrepreneur, I have produced this book in addition to other written works, merchandise and art etc. Back in 2017, I released part one of the epic fantasy adventure book series title – **AGES OF RAEKWON**, which I wrote for young adults. Charting the bitter battle between the ancient forces of good over evil, book one reveals the effects on mankind, and much more. Self-published as a rough diamond version, part ones – **AWAKENINGS AROUSAL THE PEOPLES STORY**, sheds light on a time long before the first pyramid, here the worldwide battle begins. I wrote the series over several years and hope to one day, achieve investment, remaster/re-release part one, having it along with the other books in its series also brought to the light of cinema or screens as an epic weekly television series.

In June 2018, I appeared with this book and its art on television, as a dinner guest and hosting competitor, on an episode which spanned five evenings of the UK Channel 4s' – **COME AND DINE WITH ME**, programme. **(And yes, I appreciate doing interviews about my books, motivational speeches etc, therefore, if you would like to invite me onto your - radio show, into your school or on to your television show please, contact me through my website!)**

Log onto my website @ www.
iamgoingfar.com

Follow me on Social Media @

INSTAGRAM **CJ_Israel7**
YOUTUBE:
I AM GOING FAR WITH MILES PR. Also – CJ ISRAEL BOOKS

FACEBOOK:
CJ ISRAEL BOOKS.

Thanks for reading this page. Do keep in touch through my website. Warm regards, Peace, Love & Unity from *C J Israel*

'PERSONAL ACHIEVEMENT / PROGRESS CHART'

Parents/carers, on the following pages you can Record the Milestones & Precious gems of development of the special little person/s that is close to Your heart.

Choose to write/ document the various markers of Development/Progress such as: When **Young Master/s/Miss/s**...
Began -Tying shoelaces without your help. **Rode a bike without stabilisers. Stopped wetting the bed. Overcame a hurdle**, for example - ate their vegetables - took off the armbands and swam, voluntarily read this book to you or to their siblings etc, etc... they'll be pleased to know, that you can purchase

'Miles PR REWARDS' - Stickers, Sticker Books, Colouring in Books, PR Medals, Award Certificates, Trophies, Badge... for them through my

Website at **www.iamgoingfar.com**

Check out the bright colourful - **Posters, Growth Charts, Activity booklets, Greetings Cards, T-shirts and much, much more**... soon to be available - featuring cute/ fascinating depictions from this story. Make the child / children smile fizzing with pride inside at receiving these vibrant gifts from

my extensive list whether it's a birthday present or unexpected treat.

'THIS HERE IS THE

PERSONAL ACHIEVEMENT / PROGRESS CHART OF

YOUNG MASTER/s/MISS/s ....

BORN .... THIS RECORD STARTED ON ....

BY .... YOUNG MISS/S OR MASTER/S ....

ACHIEVED THE FOLLOWING

RODE A BIKE WITHOUT STABILISERS.
AT AGE/S .... DATE/S ....
WHERE
....

STOPPED WETTING THE BED.
AT AGE/S .... DATE/S ....
WHERE...

OVERCAME A HURDLE I.E. ATE THEIR VEGETABLES
THEIR ACTUAL HURDLE/S
....
....
AT AGE/S................................ DATE/S ....
WHERE..

TOOK OFF THE ARMBANDS.
& INDEPENDENTLY SWAM
AT AGE/S ....
DATE/S .... WHERE
....
....

੧੩੩

DID SOMETHING AMAZING TO HELP SOMEONE.

AT AGE/S .... DATE/S

WHAT IT WAS & WHERE THIS HAPPENED

I AM GOING FAR

WITH MILES PЯ

VOLUNTARILY READ THIS BOOK

TO ....

AT AGE/S .... DATE/S ....

WHERE ....

LOST A TOP OR BOTTOM FRONT TOOTH

AT AGE/S .... DATE/S ....

WHERE ....

SPREAD THEIR BED FOR THEMSELVES.

AT AGE/S .... DATE/S

WHERE ....

STARTED TO DO THEIR HOMEWORK.

WITHOUT BEING ASKED

AT AGE/S ....

DATE/S

WHERE ....

PЯ

A MOMENT OF FAME OR OTHER IMPORTANT MOMENT

OF ....

....

....

AT AGE/s......... DATE/s.........
WHAT WAS IT & WHERE
DID IT HAPPEN?

....

....

HERE YOU CAN WRITE
IN OTHER ACHIEVEMENTS,
PERTAINING TO
YOUNG MASTER'S / MISS'S

....

....

....

....

"SQUAWK, SQUAWK
– YOU'VE DONE AN
AMAZING JOB!"

GOODY, GOODY GANG

KEY WORD'S & SENTENCES

PLEASE   NICE   SUPER   V.I.P   GUESTS
ROLE MODEL FABULOUS   SMILE   BRAVE
KNIGHTED   POSITIVE   AWESOME   AMAZING
PERSONAL   ADORABLE   ENCOURAGE   ADVENTURE
BECOME   IMPRESS   CONDOR   HELP

BEST   TEST   GLAMOUROUS COCKATOO

EXCELLENT BEHAVIOUR   GOING FAR   TOGETHER

CONQUERORS BOOGALOO (A LATIN AMERICAN DANCE AND SONG)   REACHING
THE SKIES

SHARING   LAMBRO-GHINI (MILES'S SPORTS CAR THAT FITS ALL HIS FRIENDS)

FLYING HIGH   GOOD, GOODY GANG   GUIDE
    LEARNING

NOT SLIDE   CERTIFICATES   HOPES AND DREAMS

BELIEVE   GOLDEN RULE   EXCELLENT   AWARDS

ACHIEVE   BE YOUR BEST   BEHAVIOUR
    DESERVES

MEDALS   BRILLIANT   GOOD GUIDES   CROWN

LOOK UP   I CAN SO I AM   INCREDIBLE   TEST

BECOMING OUR BEST   MILES   ABOVE

REMARKABLE   KIND   SHARE   CARE

AMAZE   SUPER FABULOUS   GIVE   GOOD MORALES

LOOK OUT FOR EACH OTHER   GO THAT EXTRA MILE AND SMILE.

DON'T BE CRUEL   REMEMBER OUR MANNERS

As a Goodwill gesture from me the author, to further inspire greatness in ALL children,

please note that from December7th 2021, that the – I AM GOING FAR, gloss covered paperback storybook currently retailing at its revised full price of **£12.97 RRP,** due to worldwide increased paper, printing and publishing costs, will have **£0.20p/20 GB pence** of this full price, deducted following its purchase. As a donation this will later be contributed to my unique – '**I AM GOING FAR – WORLDWIDE CHILD OF EXCELLENCE IN EDUCATION FUND'. Founded by me the author C J Israel.** The fund is anticipated to be launched in late October 2021, and by December 7th, 2021, will firstly be piloted in 7 UK city schools with a view to it eventually being rolled out to certain overseas countries schools etc. Terms & Conditions apply and will be made available nearer the time through promotions, social media and online through my website. The fund's purpose is to award certain deprived children for their Much Improved; educational progress, attitude and demonstrations of having performed outstanding acts of kindness in their wider communities. Such children that usually are unable to afford a nutritious 'Hot school meal and drink' while at school, could through this fund win one paid for by me the author, other prizes may also follow too .supplied via alliances with certain big-name brand sponsors. A donation of **£0.30p/30 GB pence** taken from the sale of the velvety feel matte covered hardback storybook's full rrp price of **£15.99**, will simultaneously be donated to the fund for the same purpose.

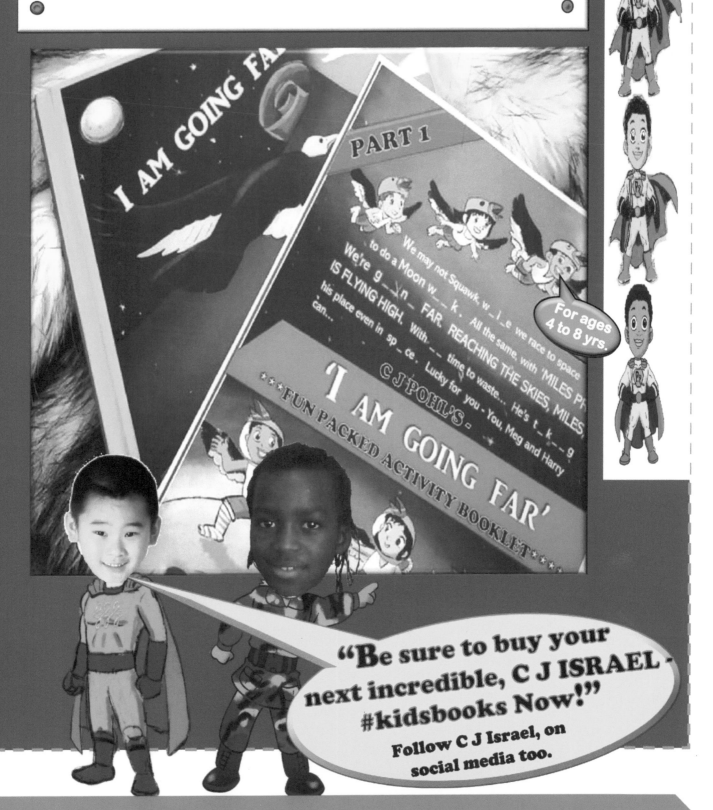

Lightning Source UK Ltd.
Milton Keynes UK
UKHW051330210421
382317UK00001B/1